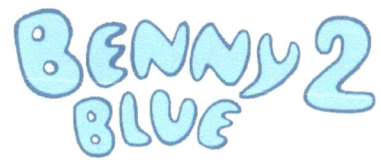

Grayscale Coloring Book
by Christine Karron

Recommended for coloring with colored pencils, markers, pens and/or crayons.
If using wet media place a sheet of thick paper or card behind the
coloring page to prevent bleed through.

All illustrations in this coloring book were originally created and
completely traditionally hand drawn by the artist Christine Karron.

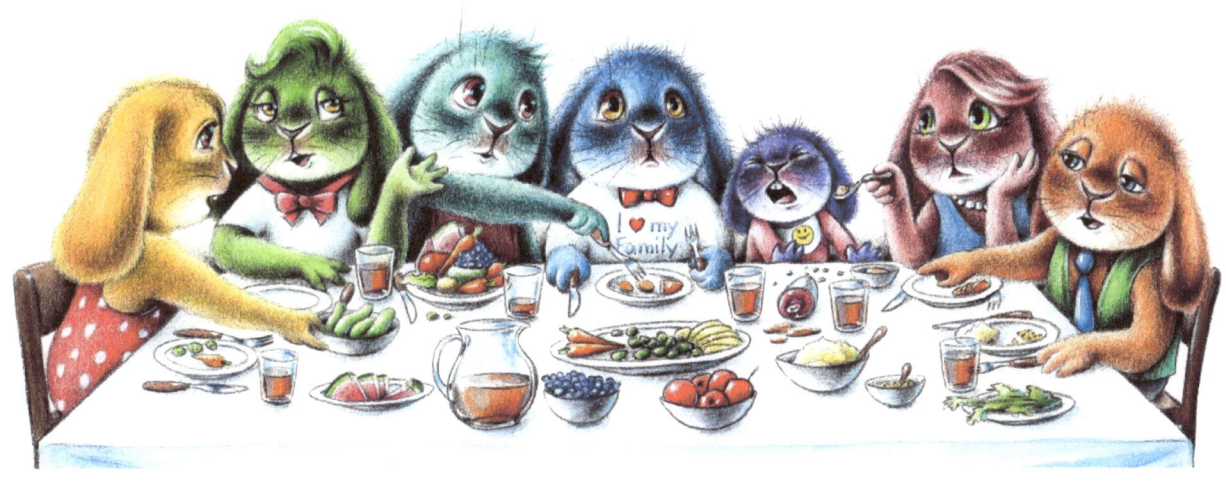

Benny Blue 2
Grayscale Coloring Book by Christine Karron
First published April 2019

ISBN: 9781095829394
Imprint: Independently published

www.chkarron.com

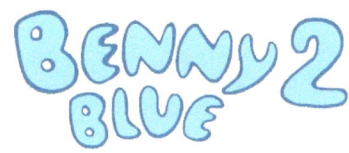

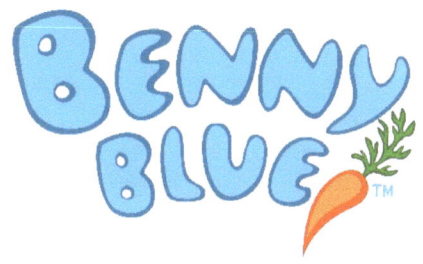

Benny Blue is a reflection of this little bit of blue in all of us.
He is a whimsical, kind-hearted, friendly, patient,
fictional character with a caring nature.
Benny Blue embraces the inner child in all of us, and puts a smile
on our faces through his everyday challenges and happenings.
With his cuteness, Benny Blue, encourages us to stay positive,
keep trying, and to make healthy choices where ever we go.
Benny Blue is a lovable bunny with a special place in our hearts.

Follow Benny Blue on Facebook and Instagram @BennyBlueBunny

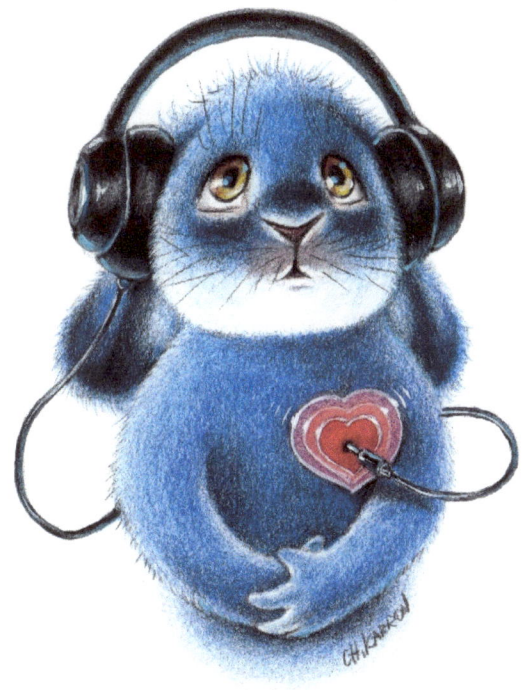

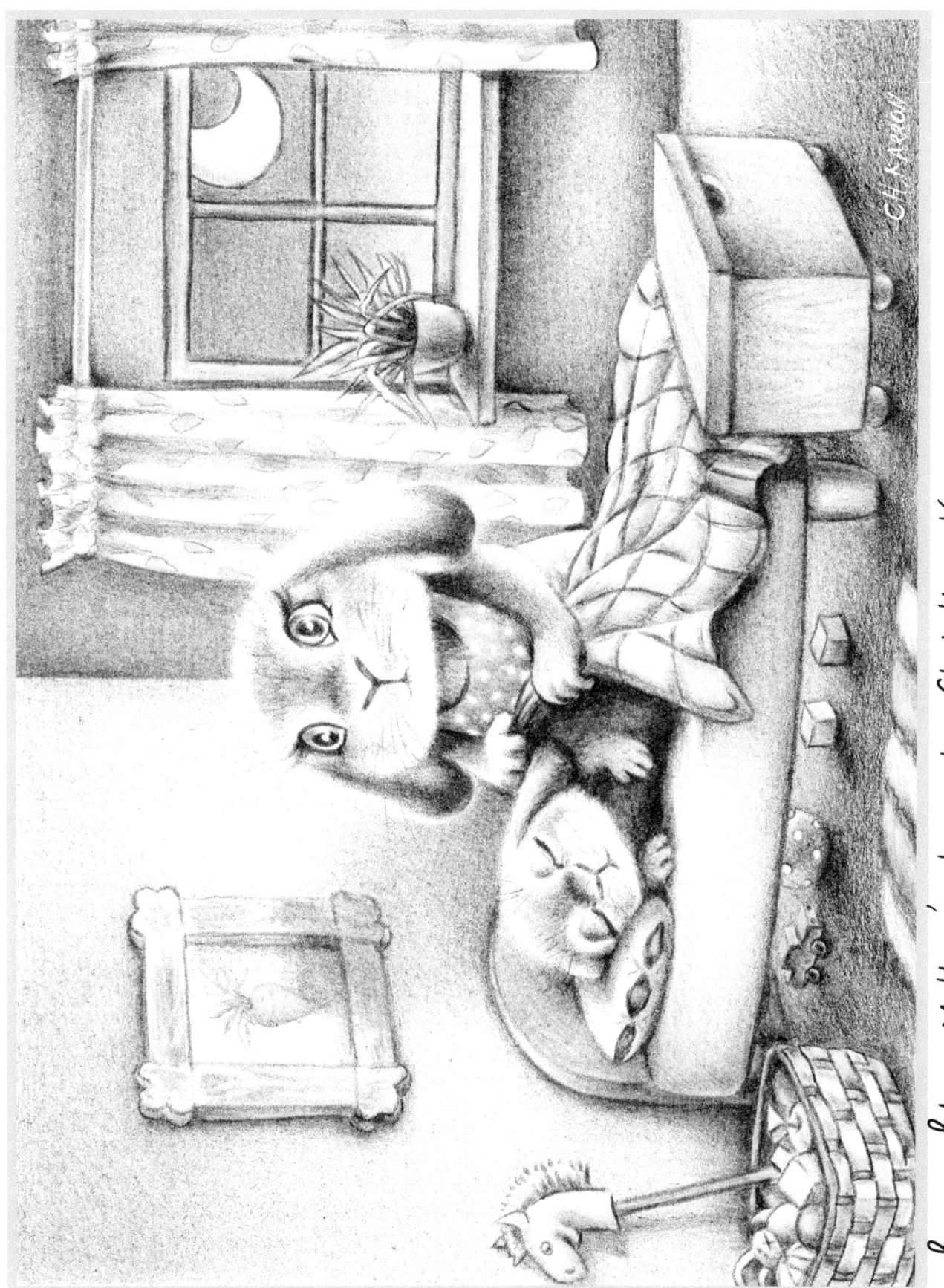

Benny Blue Mother's Love by Christine Karron

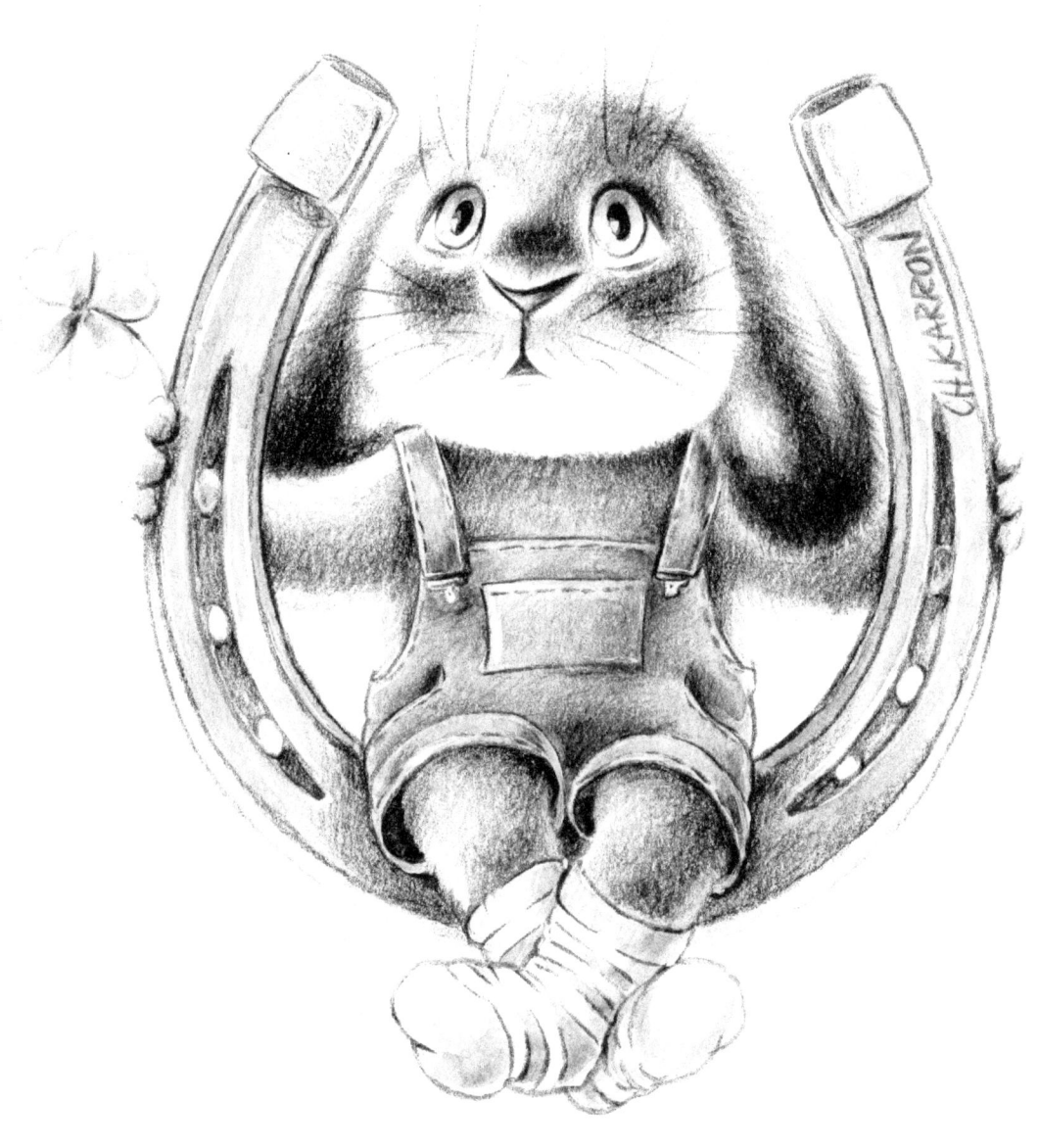

Benny Blue Lucky Horseshoe by Christine Karron

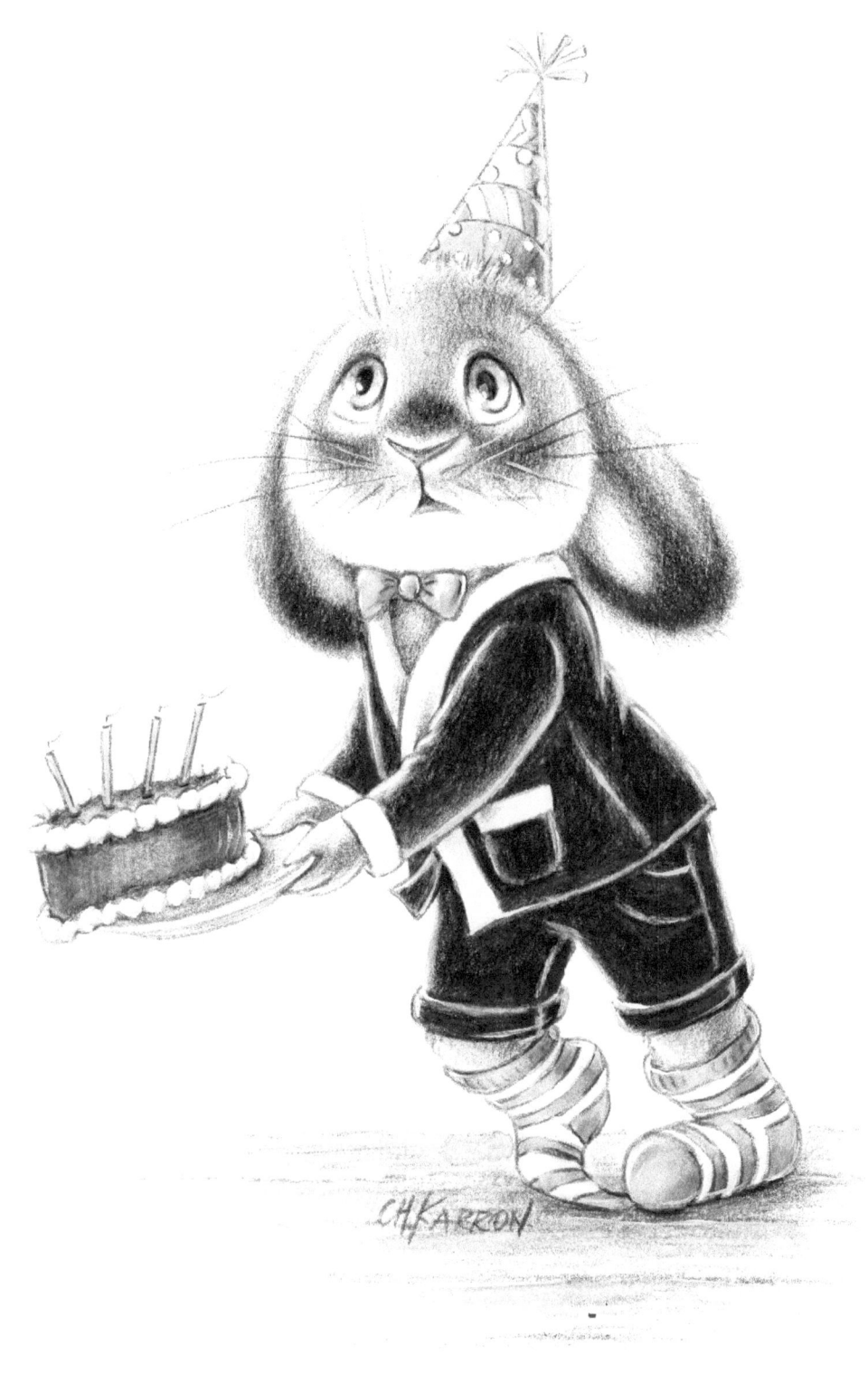

Benny Blue Birthday Cake by Christine Karron

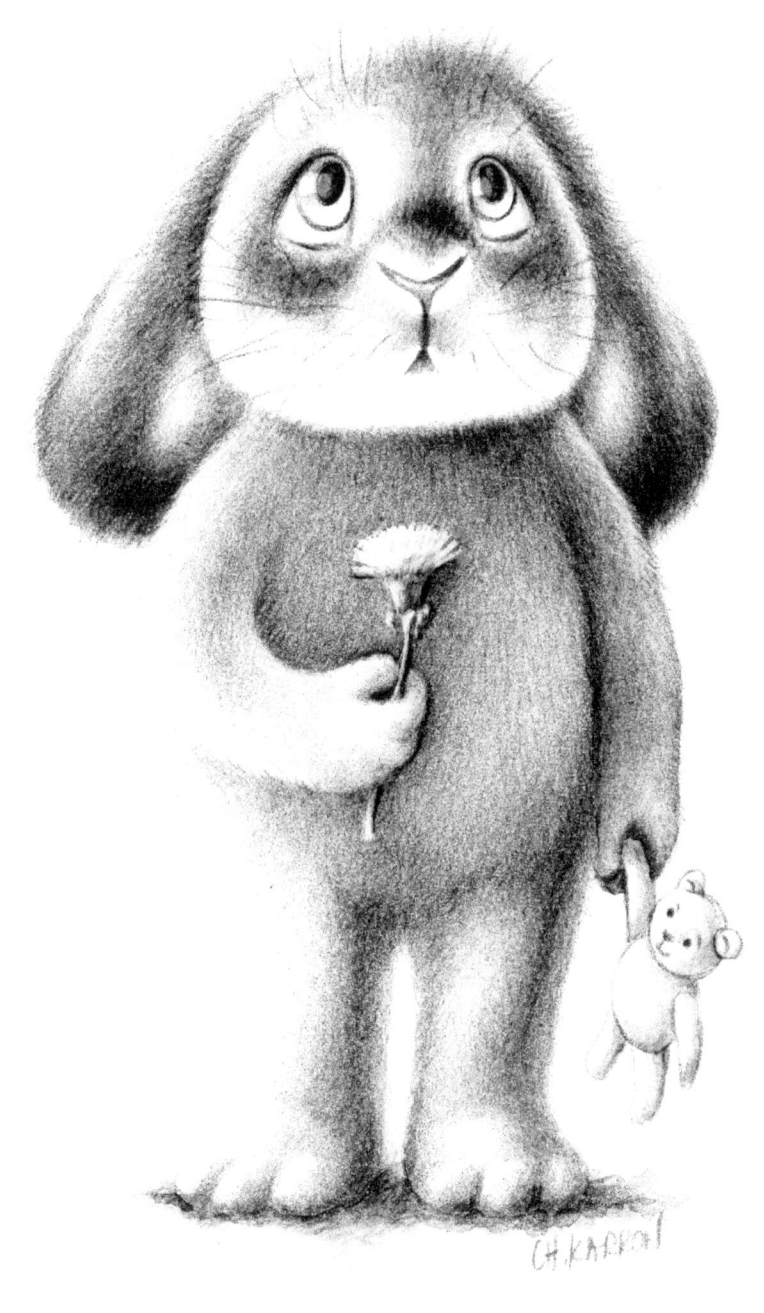

Benny Blue Sorry by Christine Karron

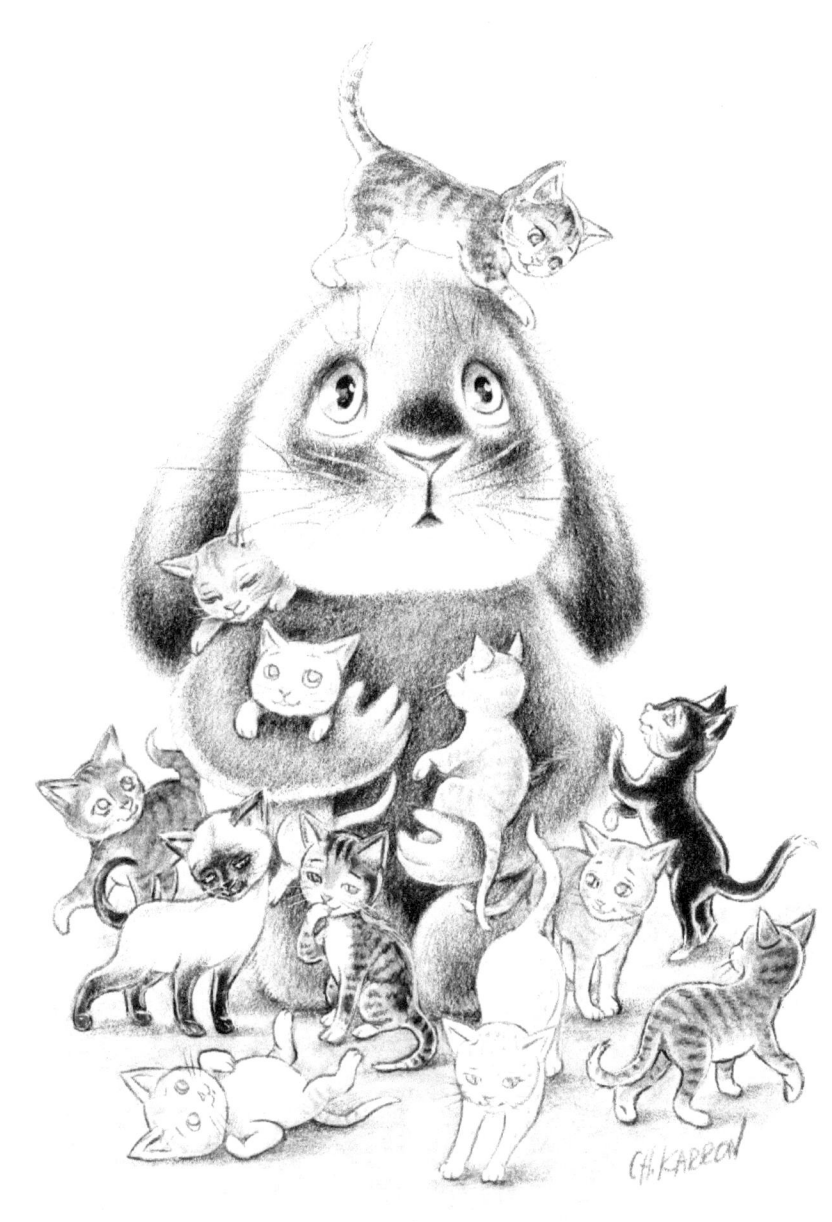

Benny Blue Kitty Sitting by Christine Karron

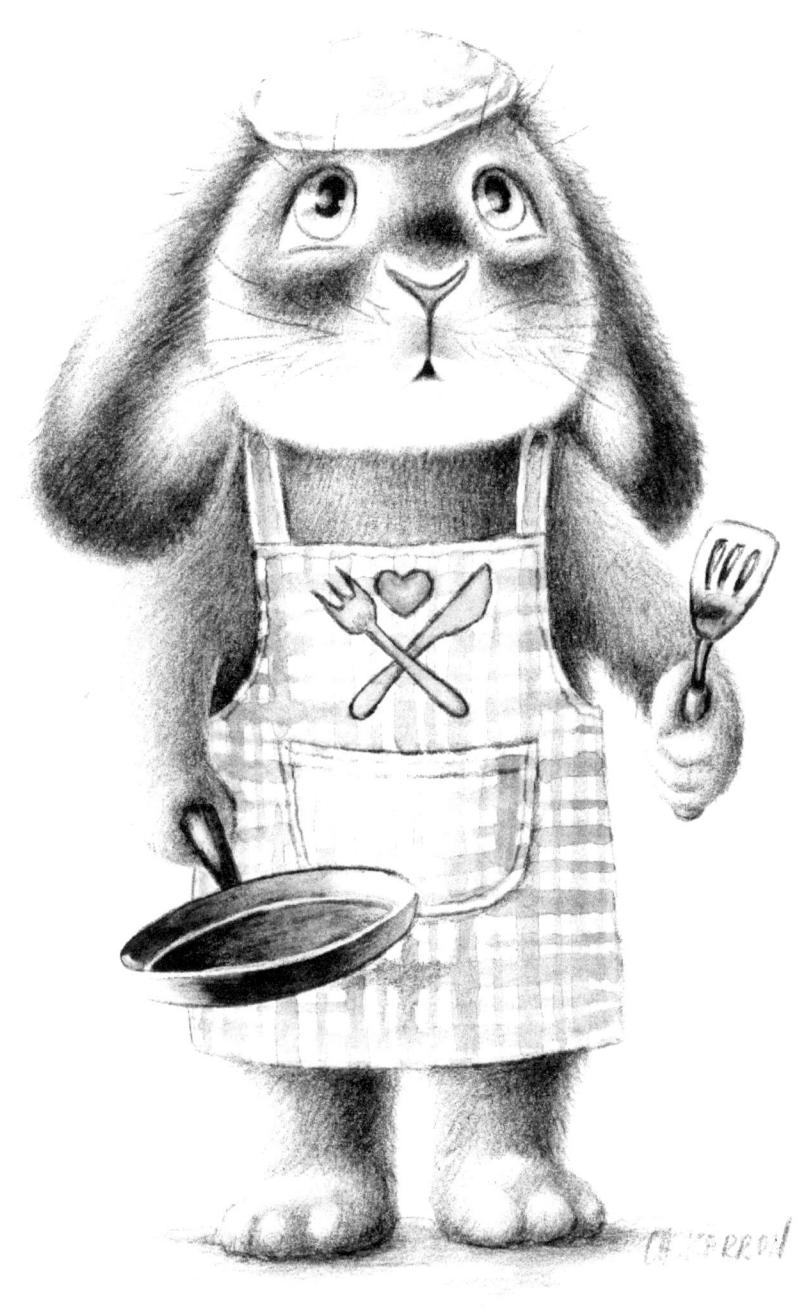

Benny Blue Pancake by Christine Karron

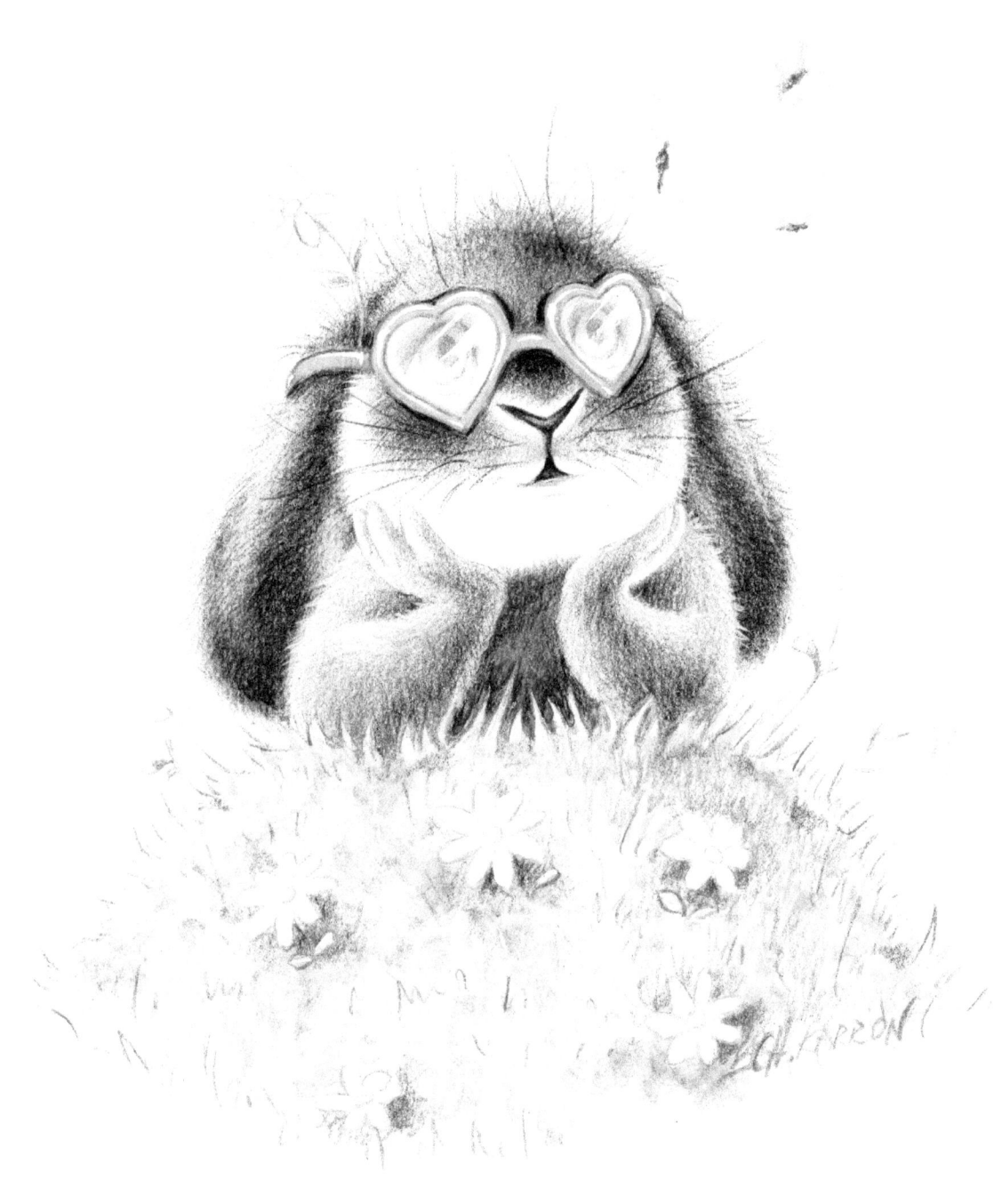

Benny Blue Pink Glasses by Christine Karron

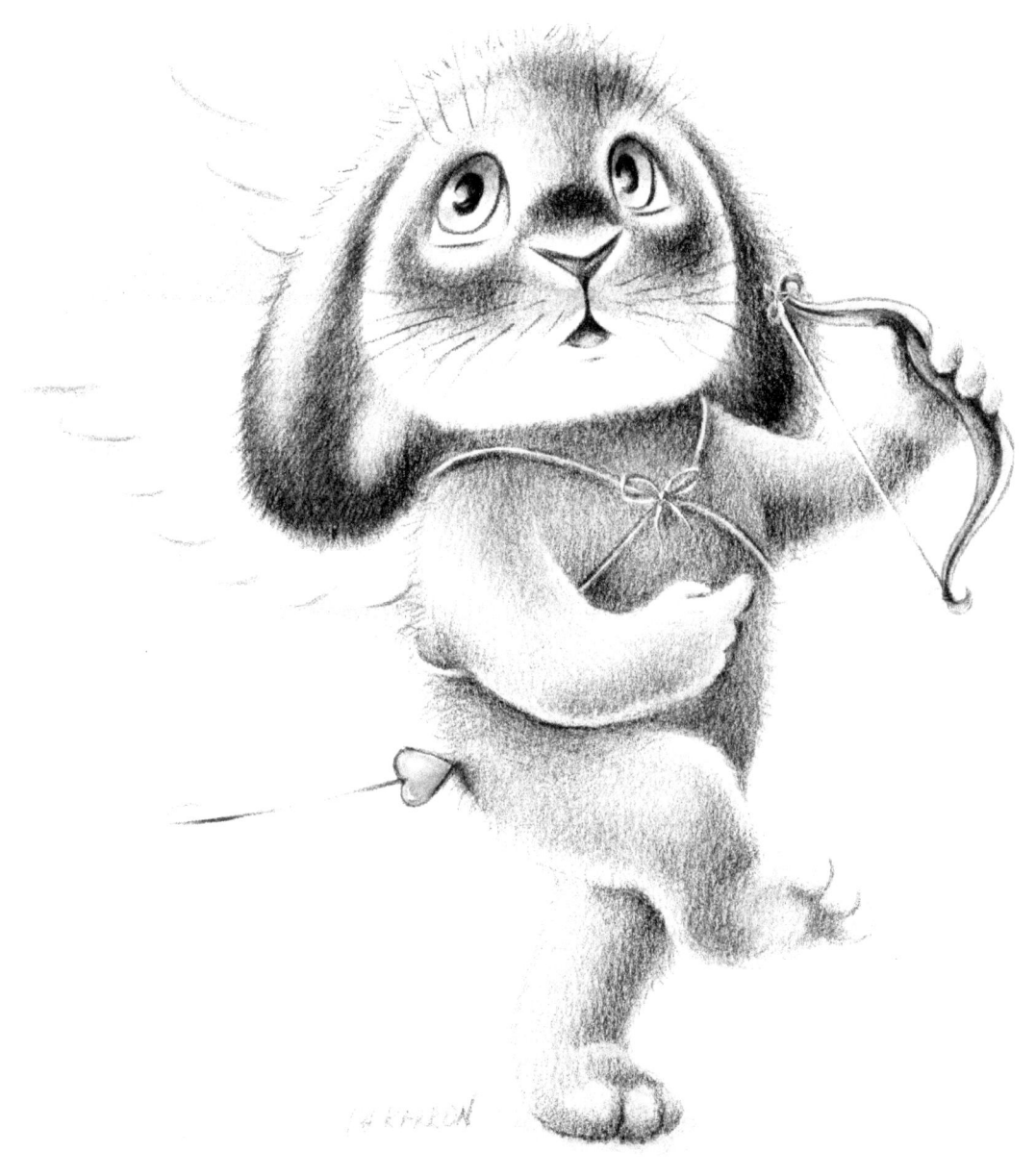

Benny Blue Amor by Christine Karron

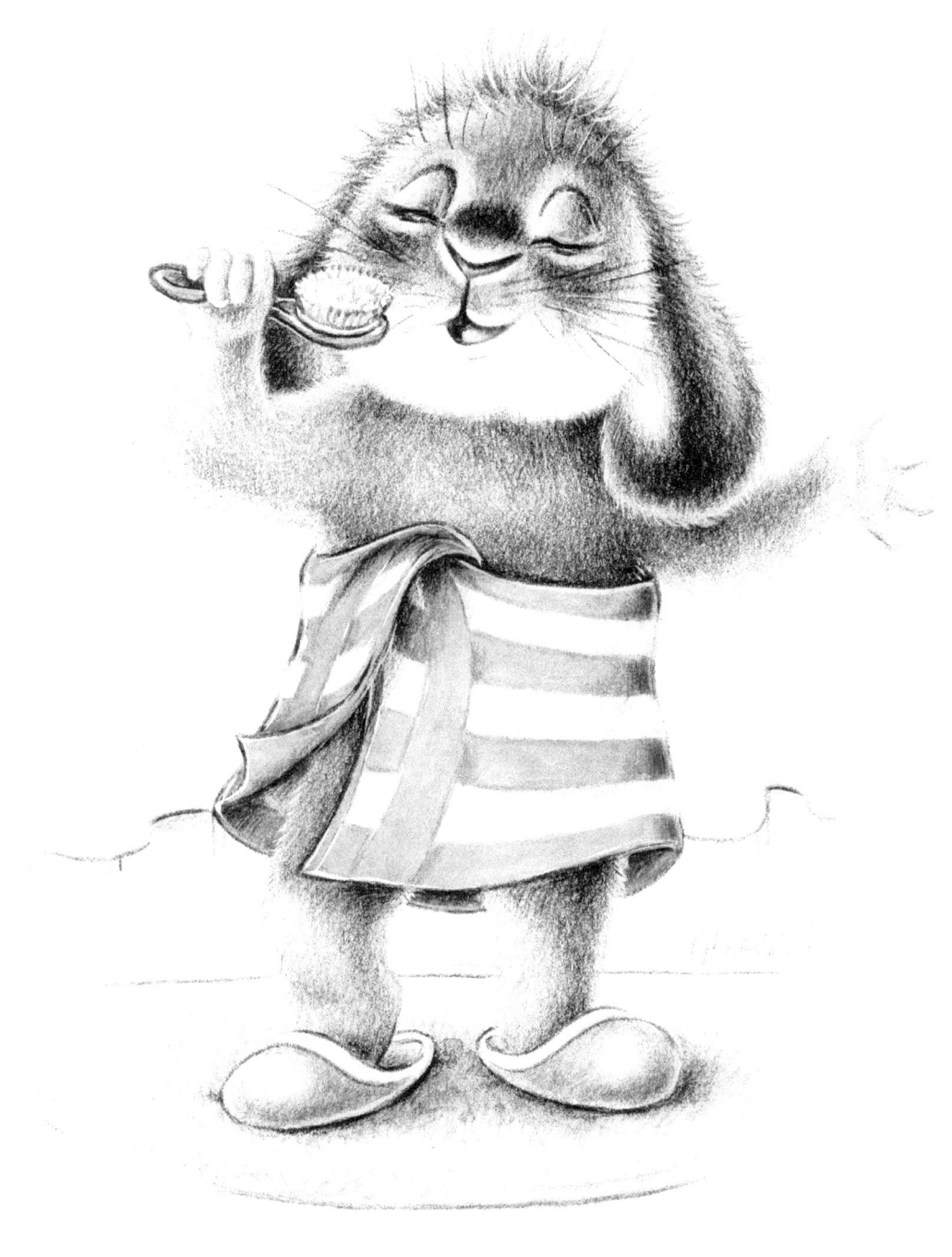

Benny Blue Bathroom Singer by Christine Karron

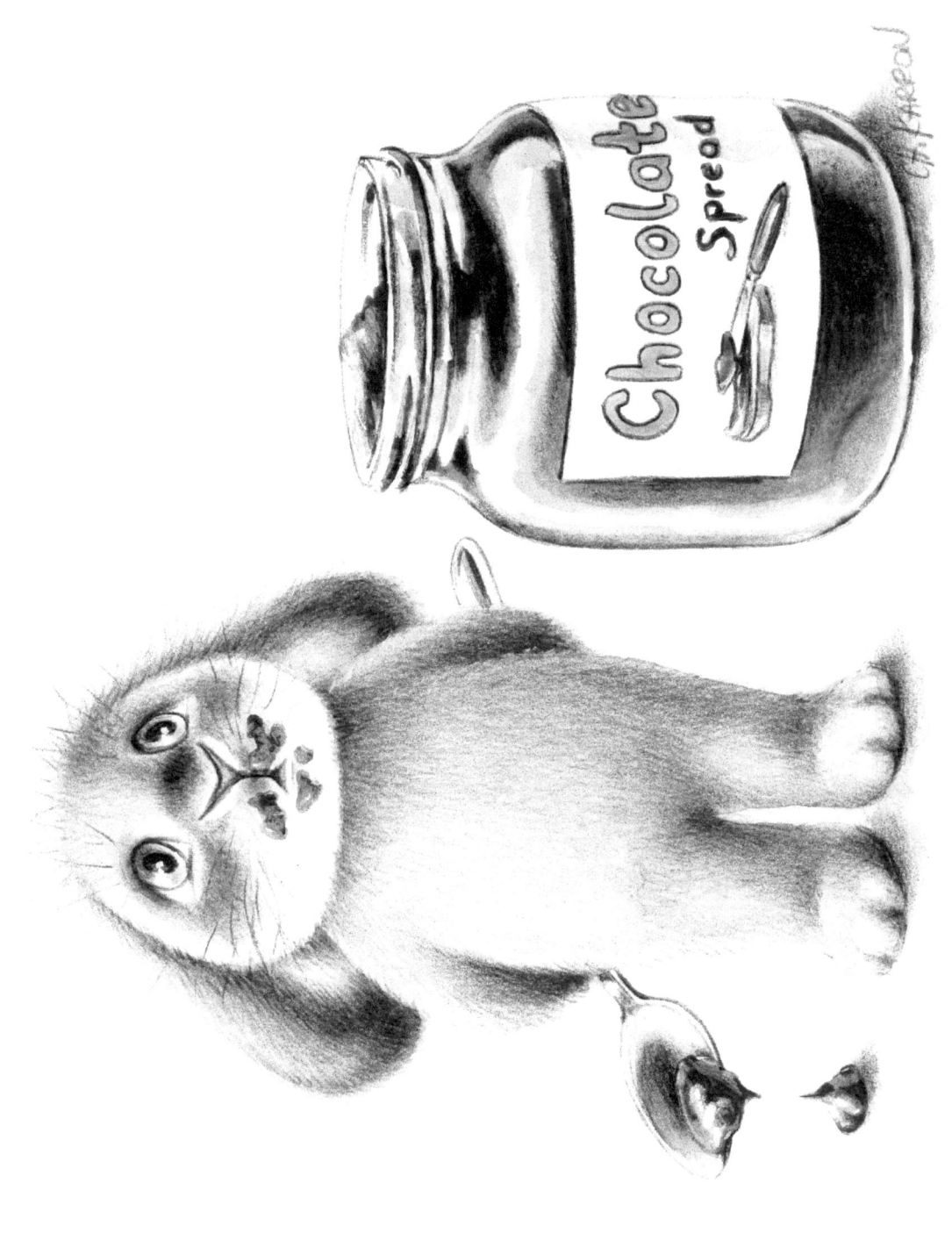

Benny Blue Spoon Of Chocolate by Christine Karron

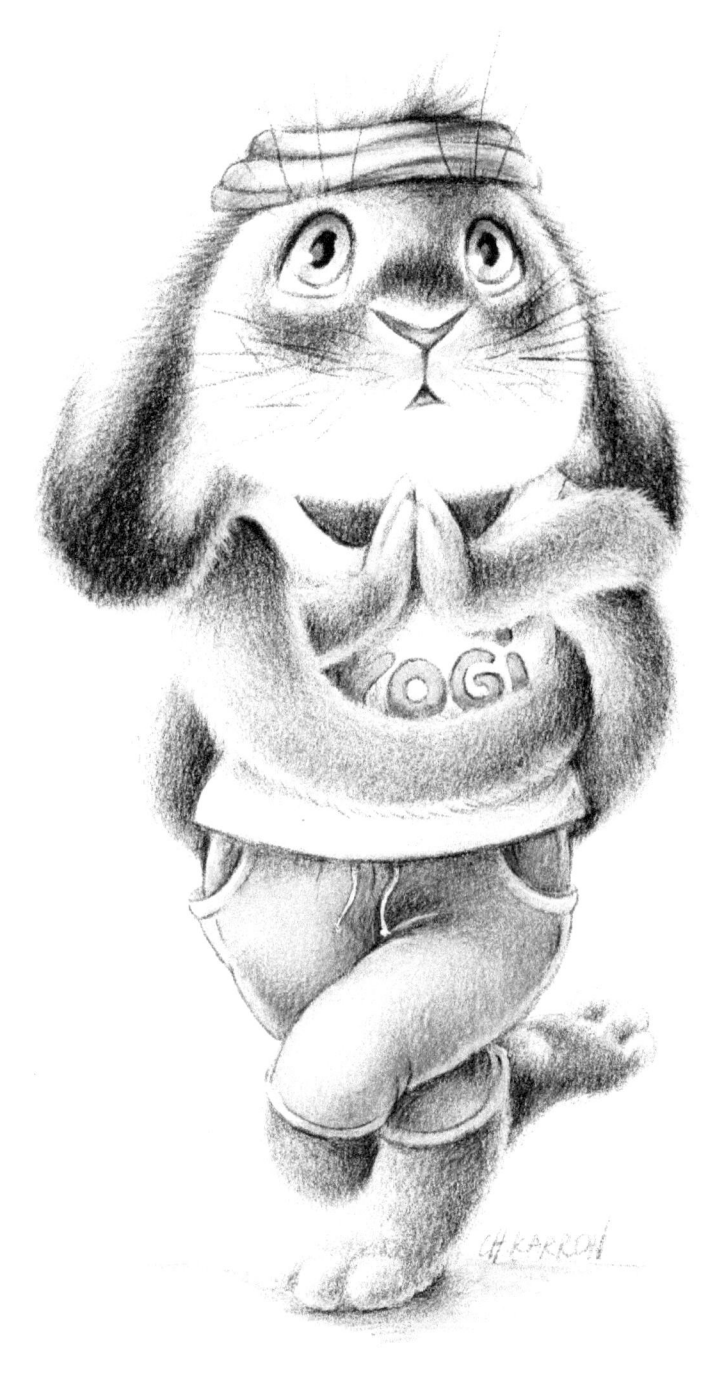

Benny Blue Yogi by Christine Karron

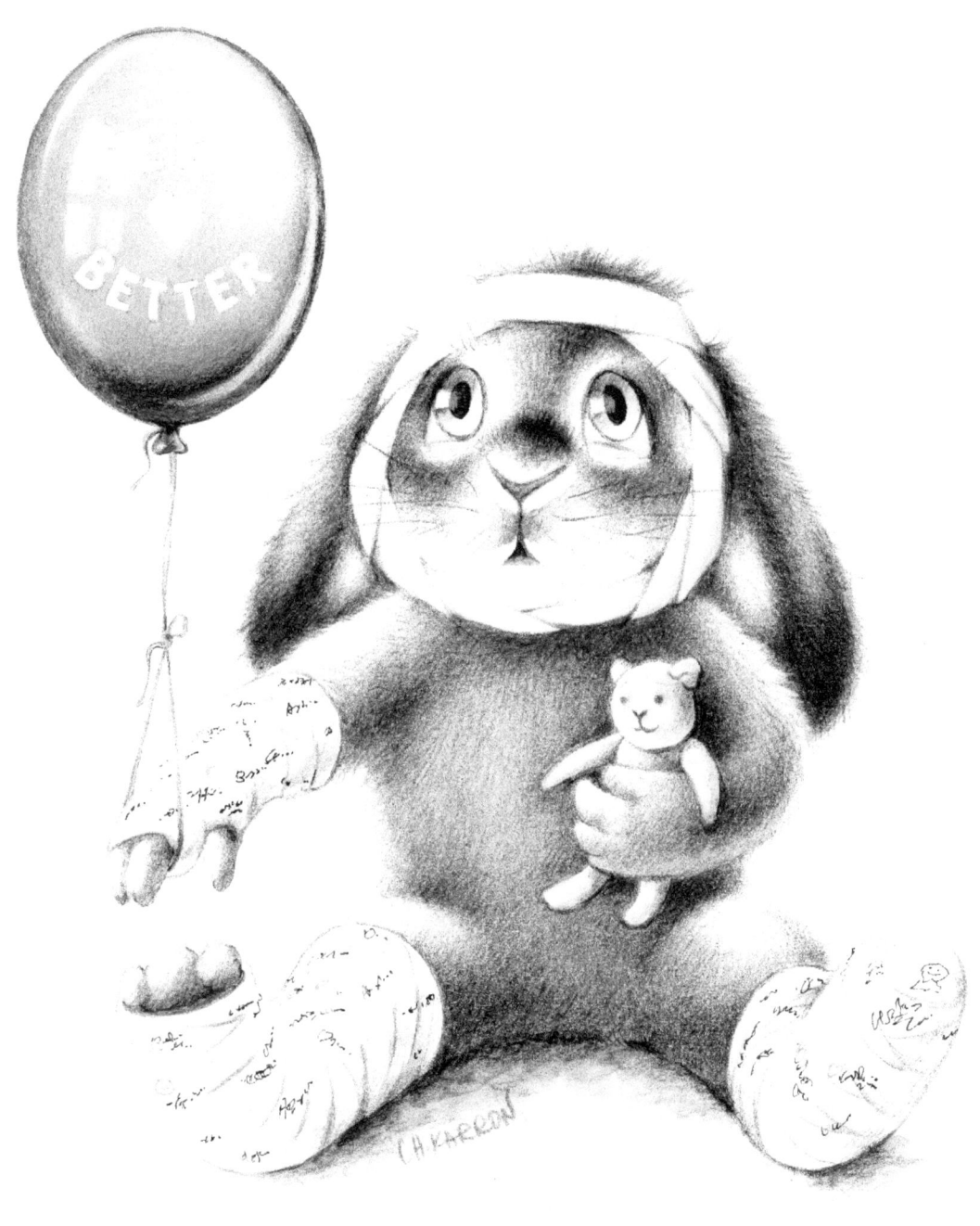

Benny Blue Feel Better by Christine Karron

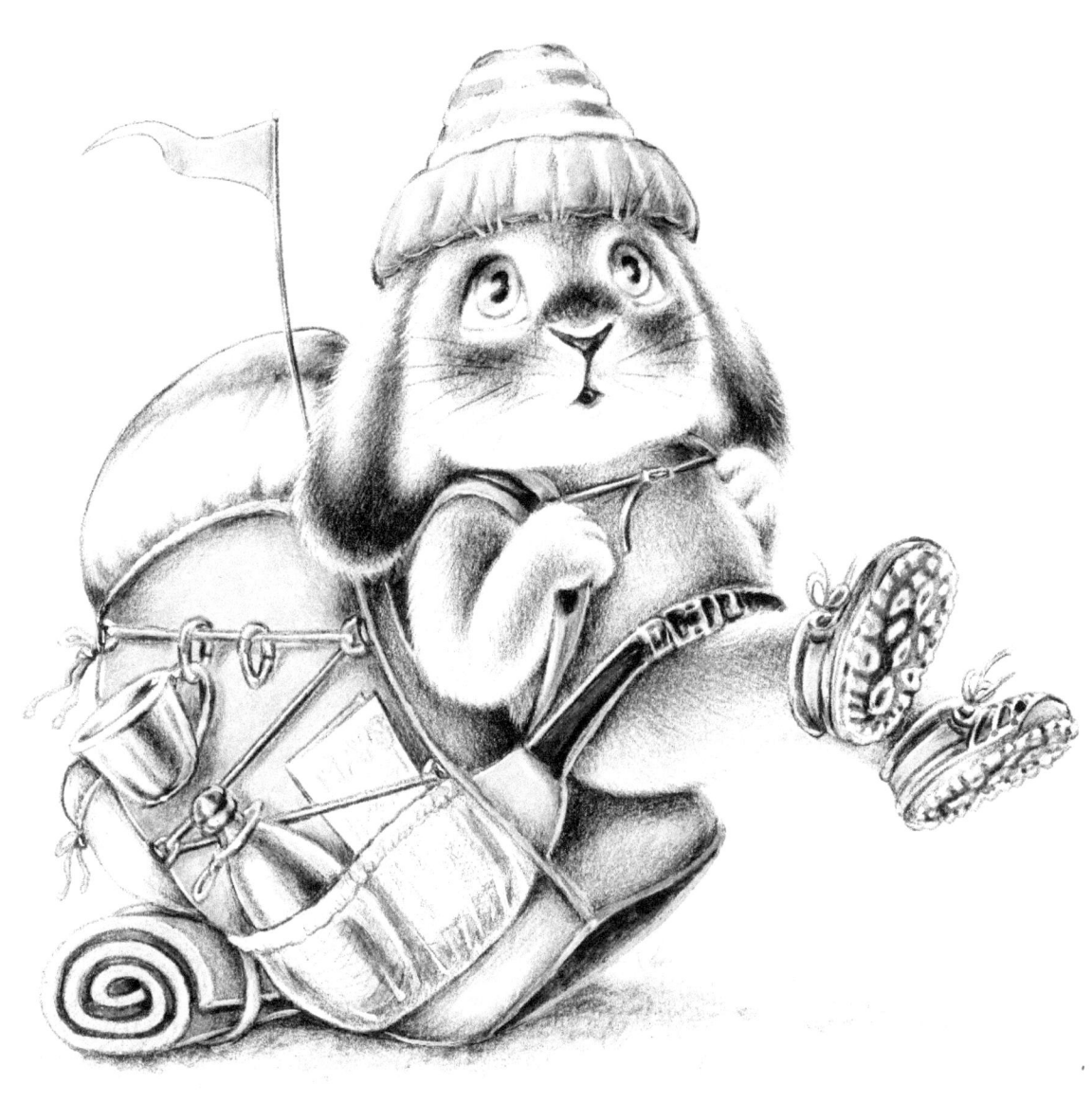

Benny Blue Backpack Hiking Adventure by Christine Karron

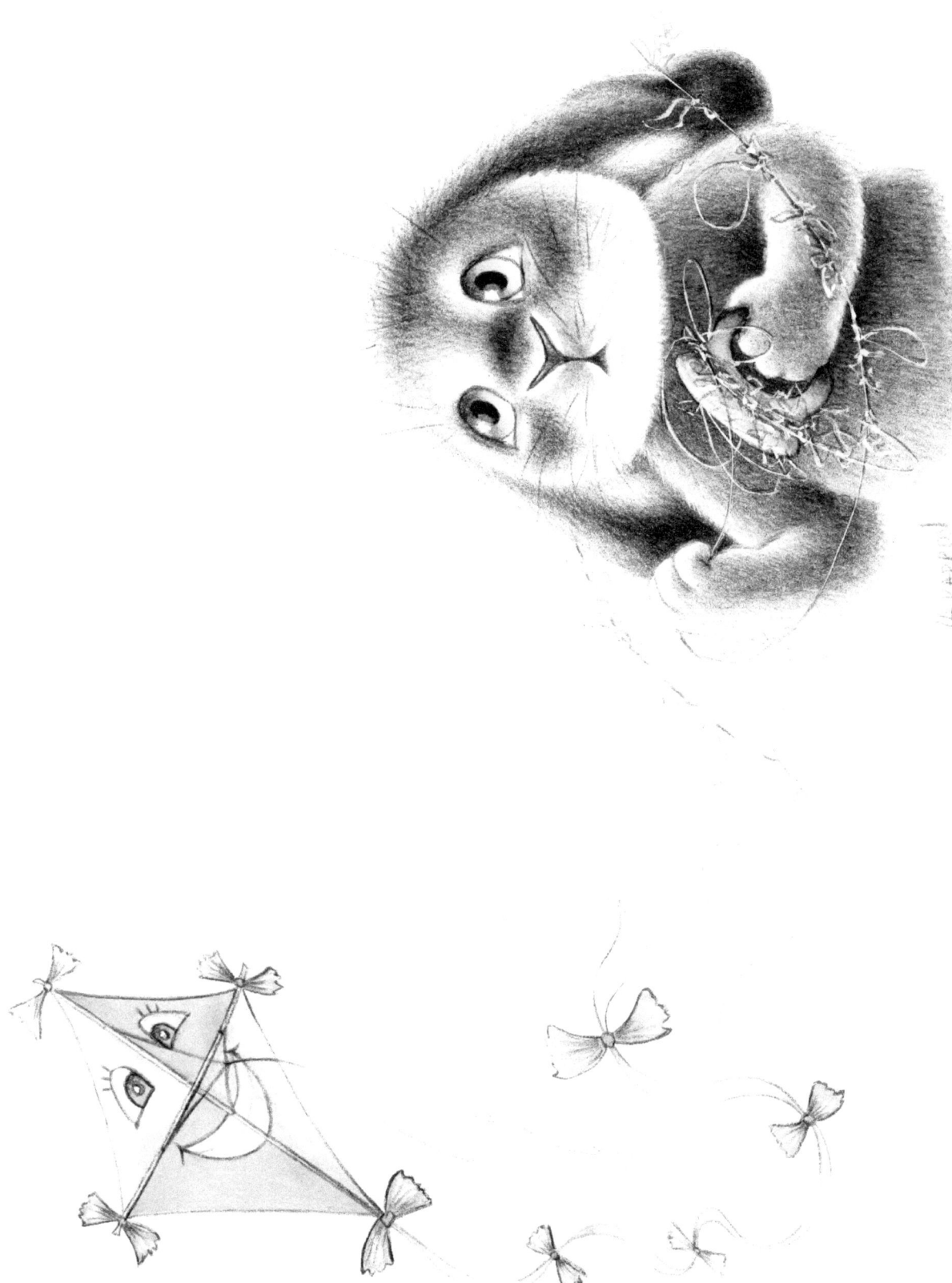

Benny Blue Kite by Christine Karron

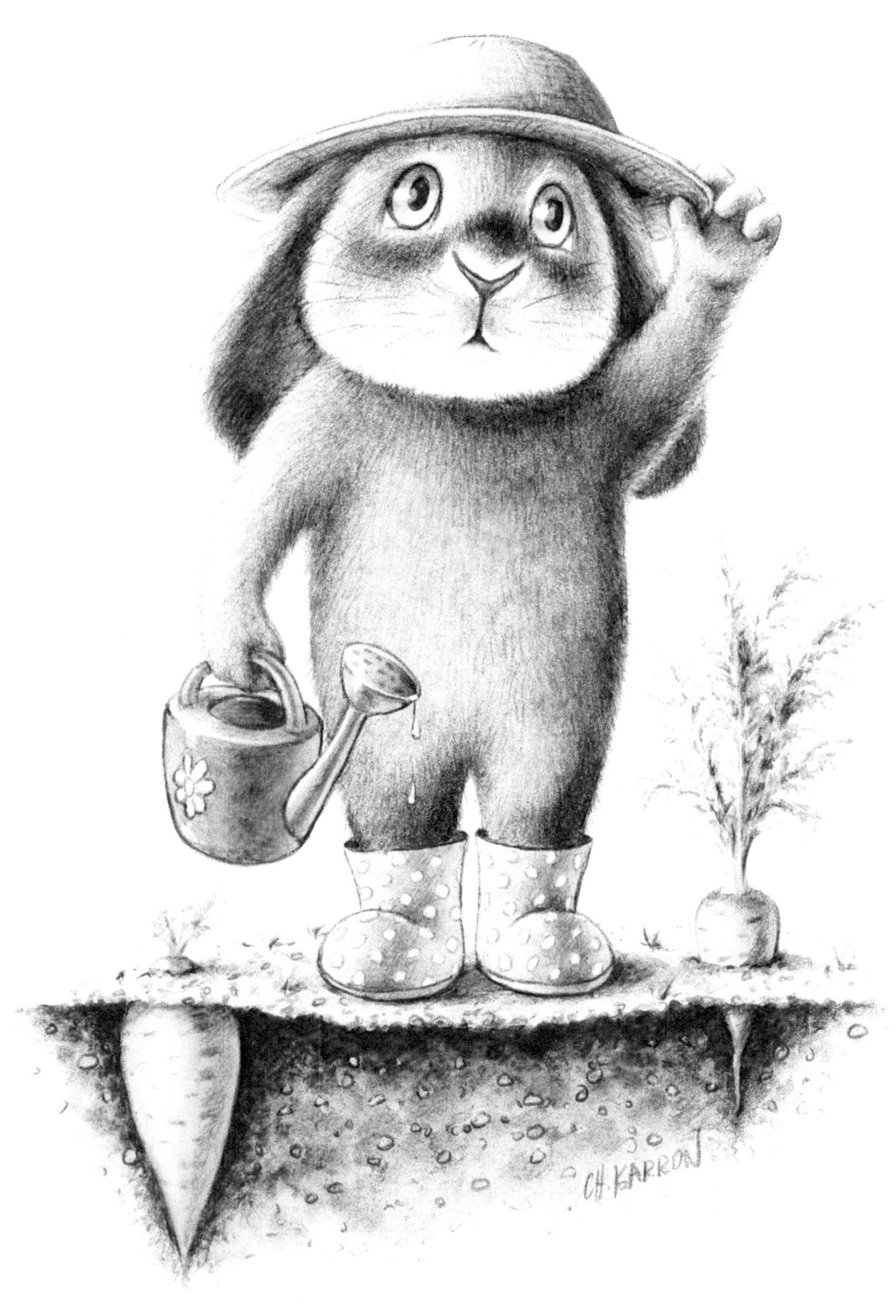

Benny Blue Gardening by Christine Karron

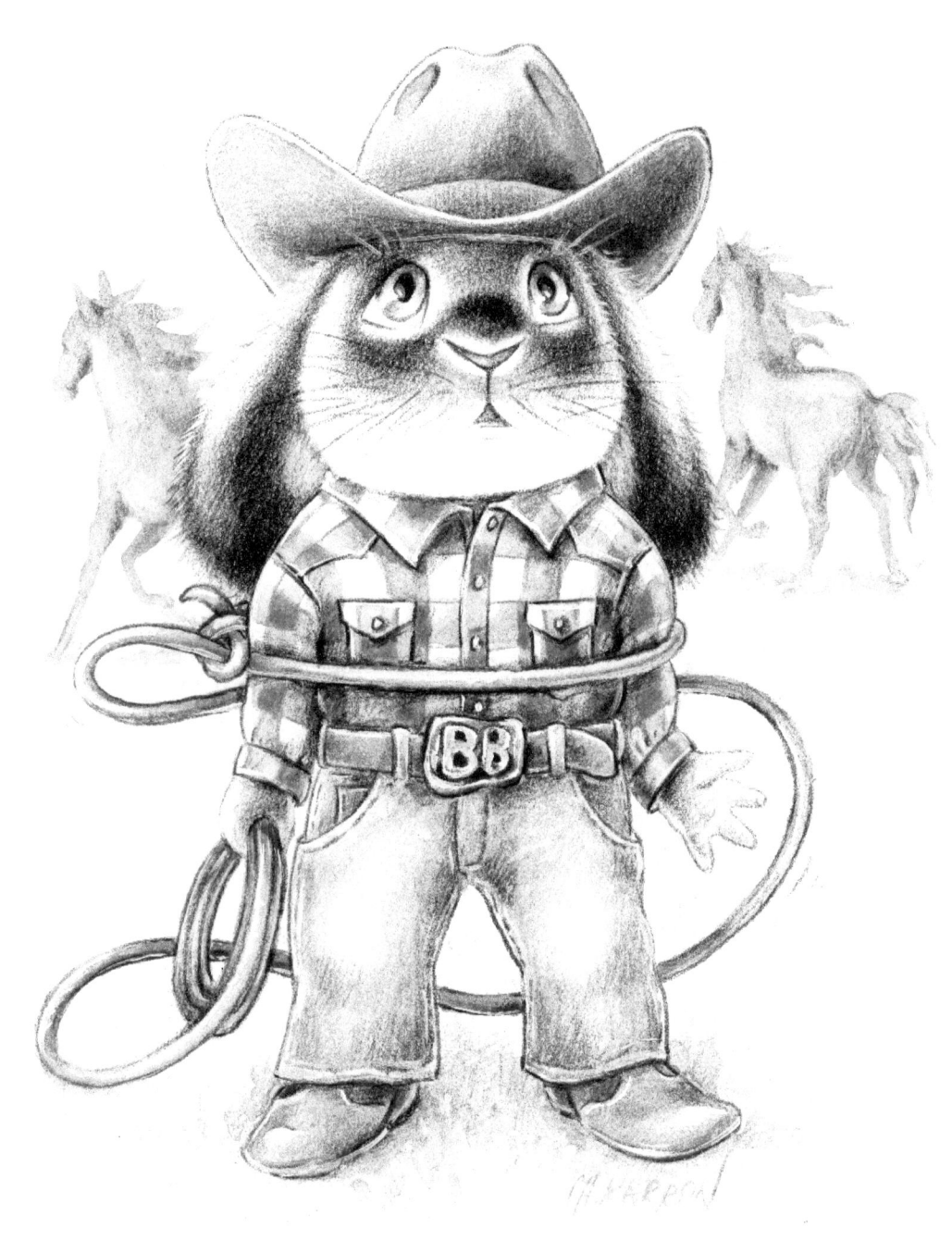

Benny Blue Cowboy Skills by Christine Karron

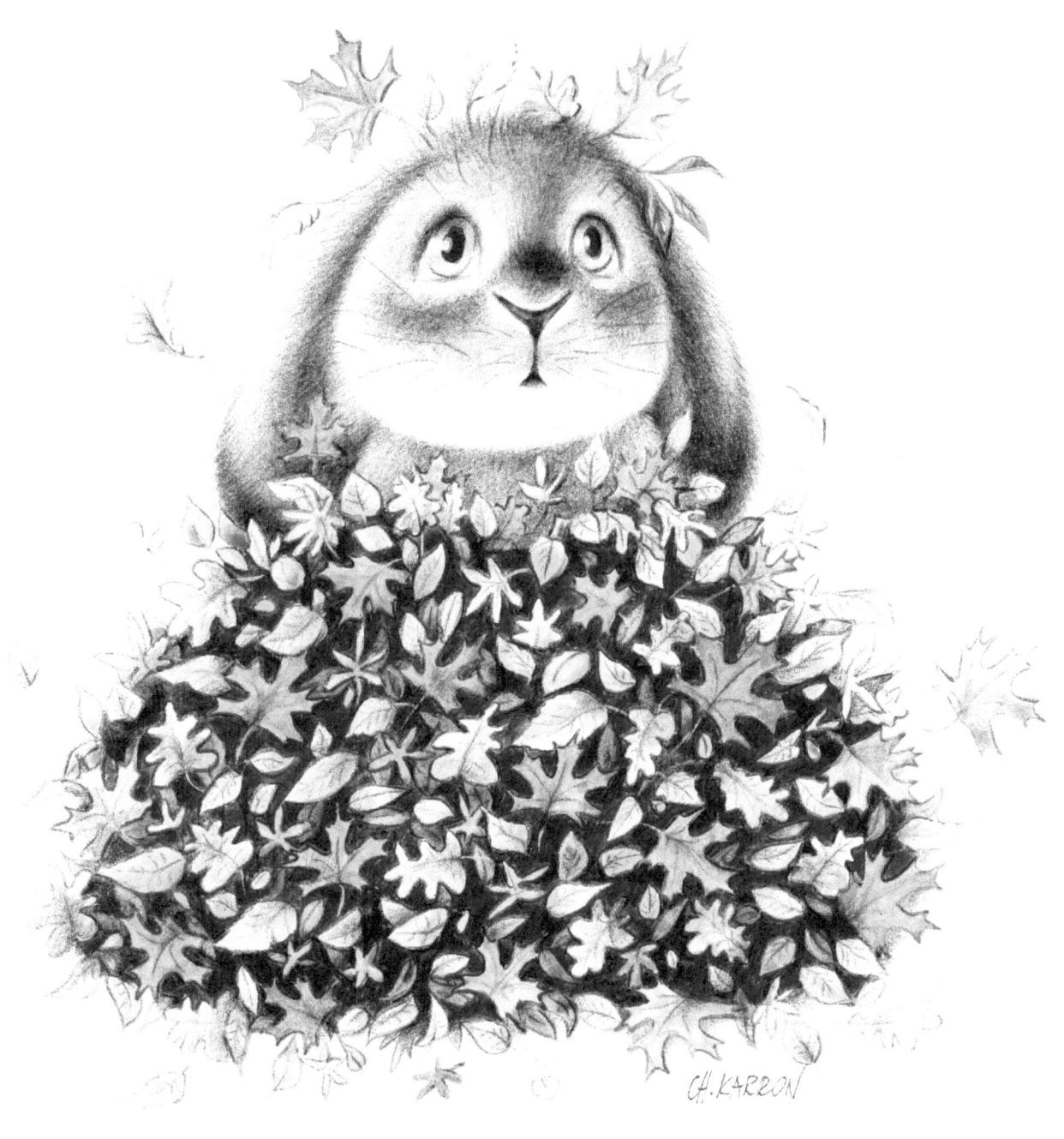

Benny Blue Leaves by Christine Karron

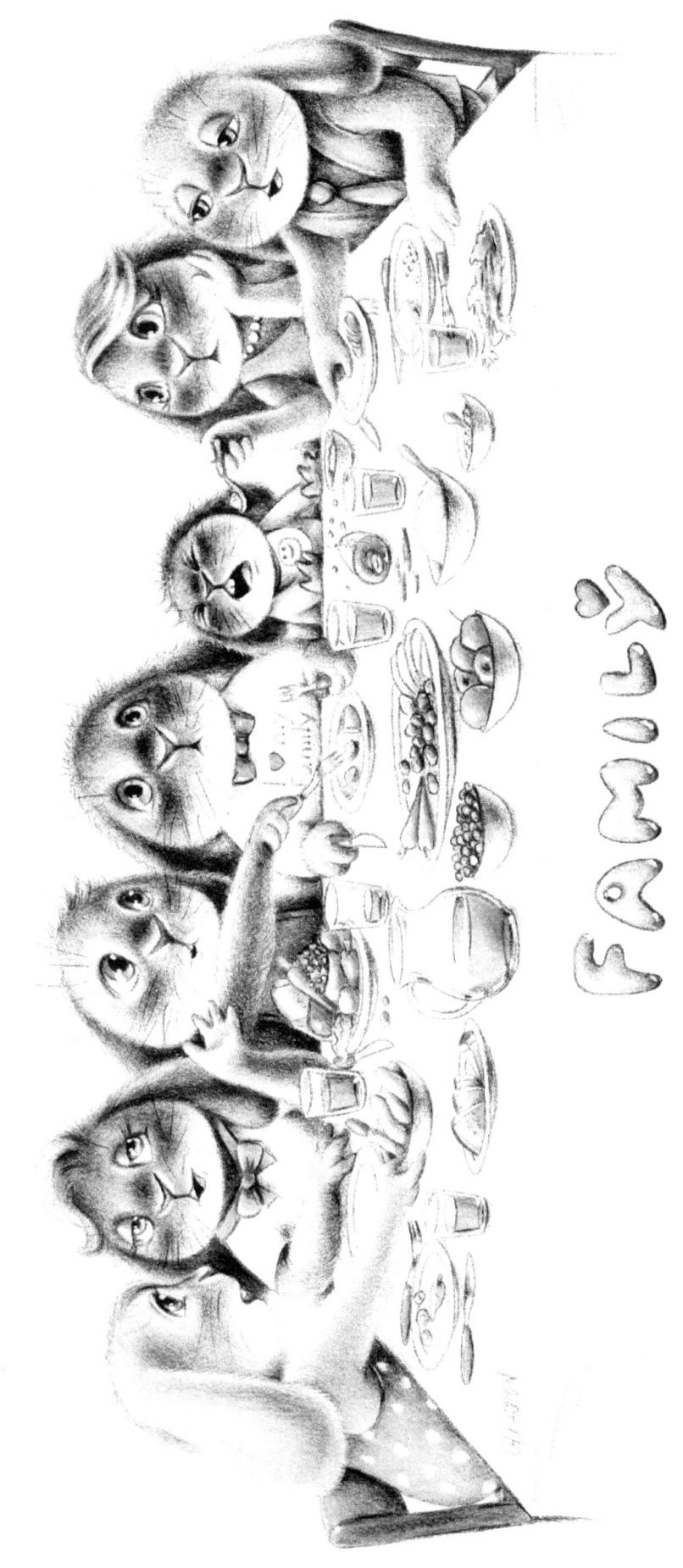

FAMILY

Benny Blue Family Dinner by Christine Karron

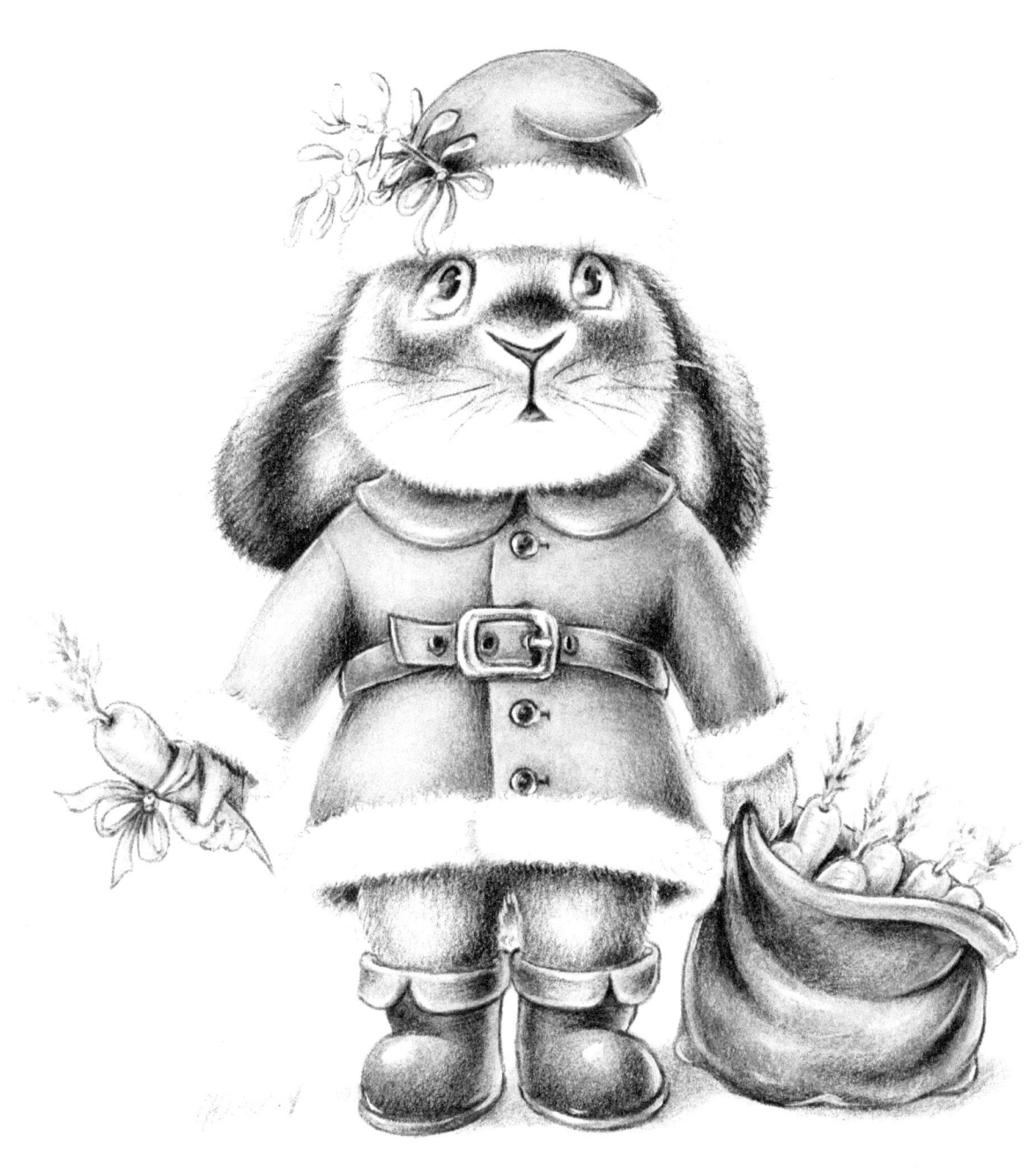

Benny Blue Santa by Christine Karron

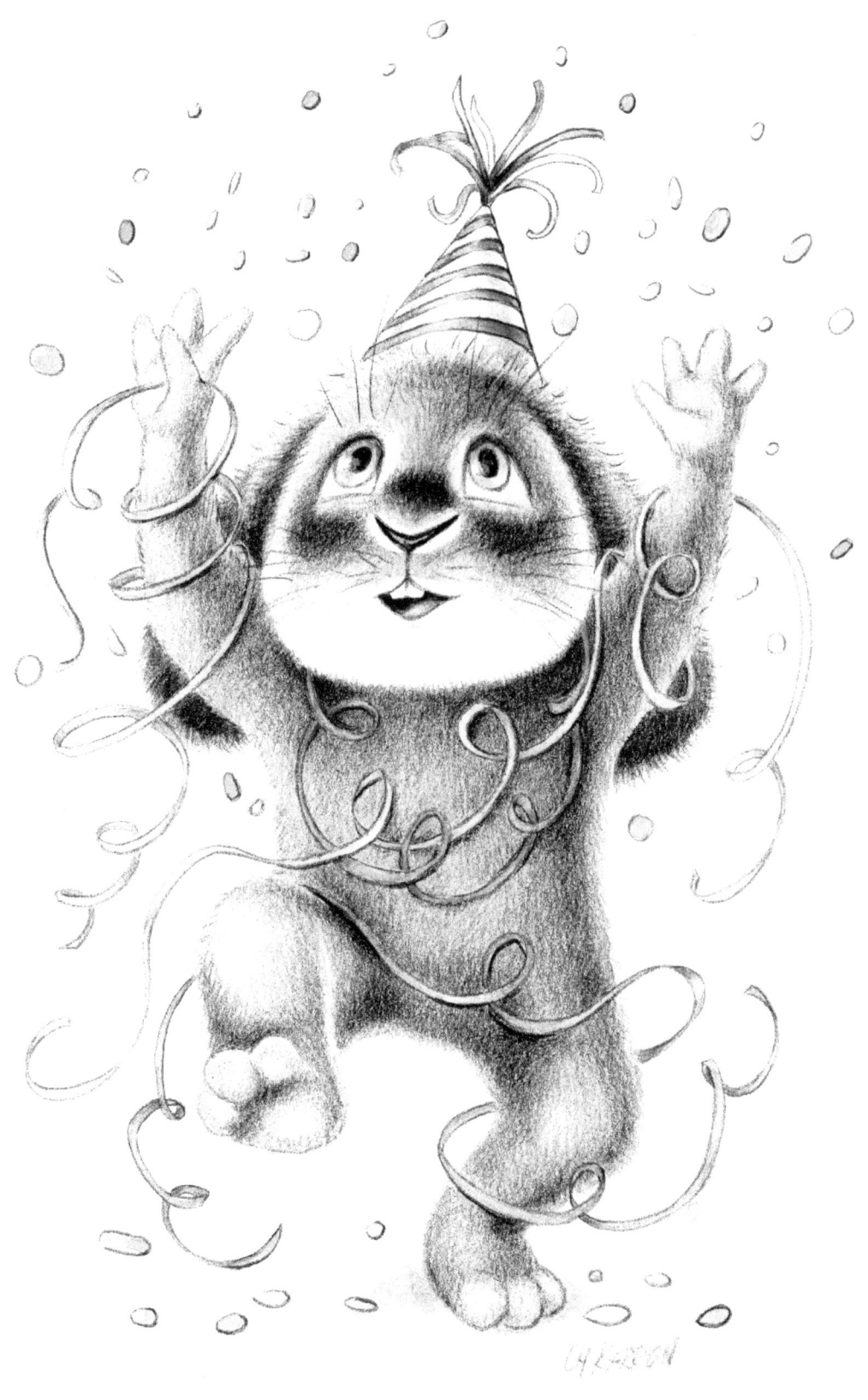

Benny Blue Celebrating by Christine Karron

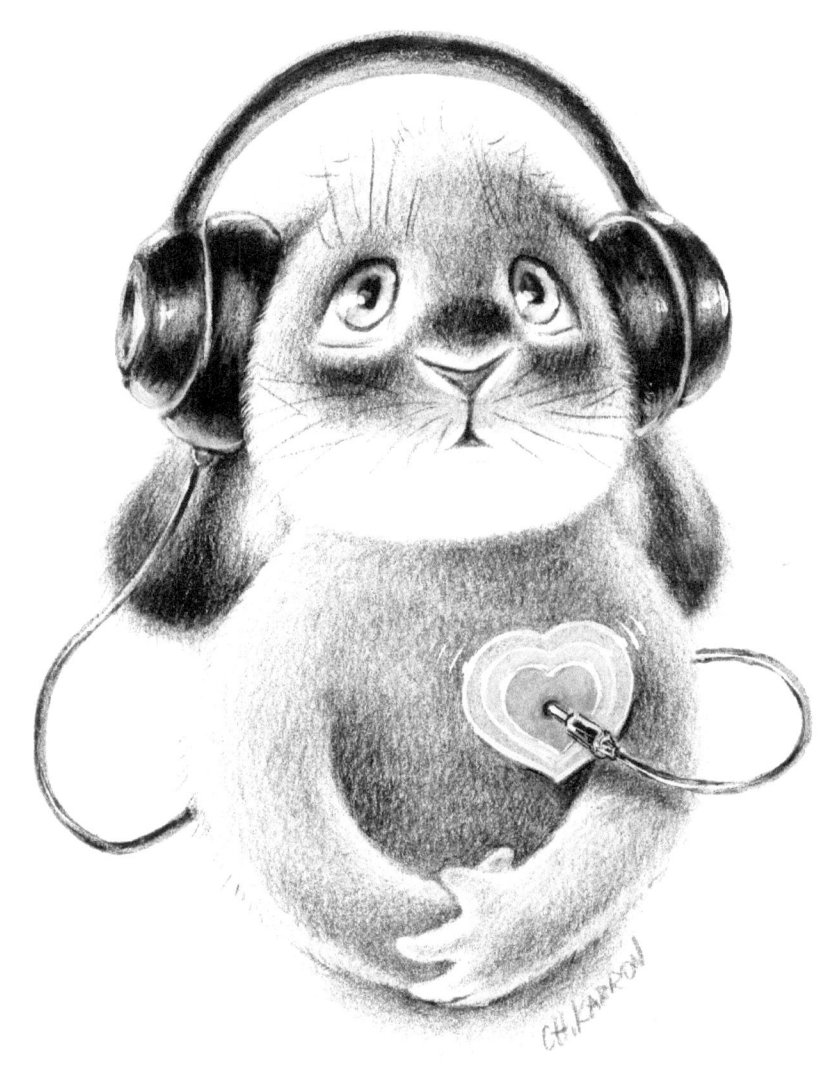

Benny Blue Listen To Your Heart by Christine Karron

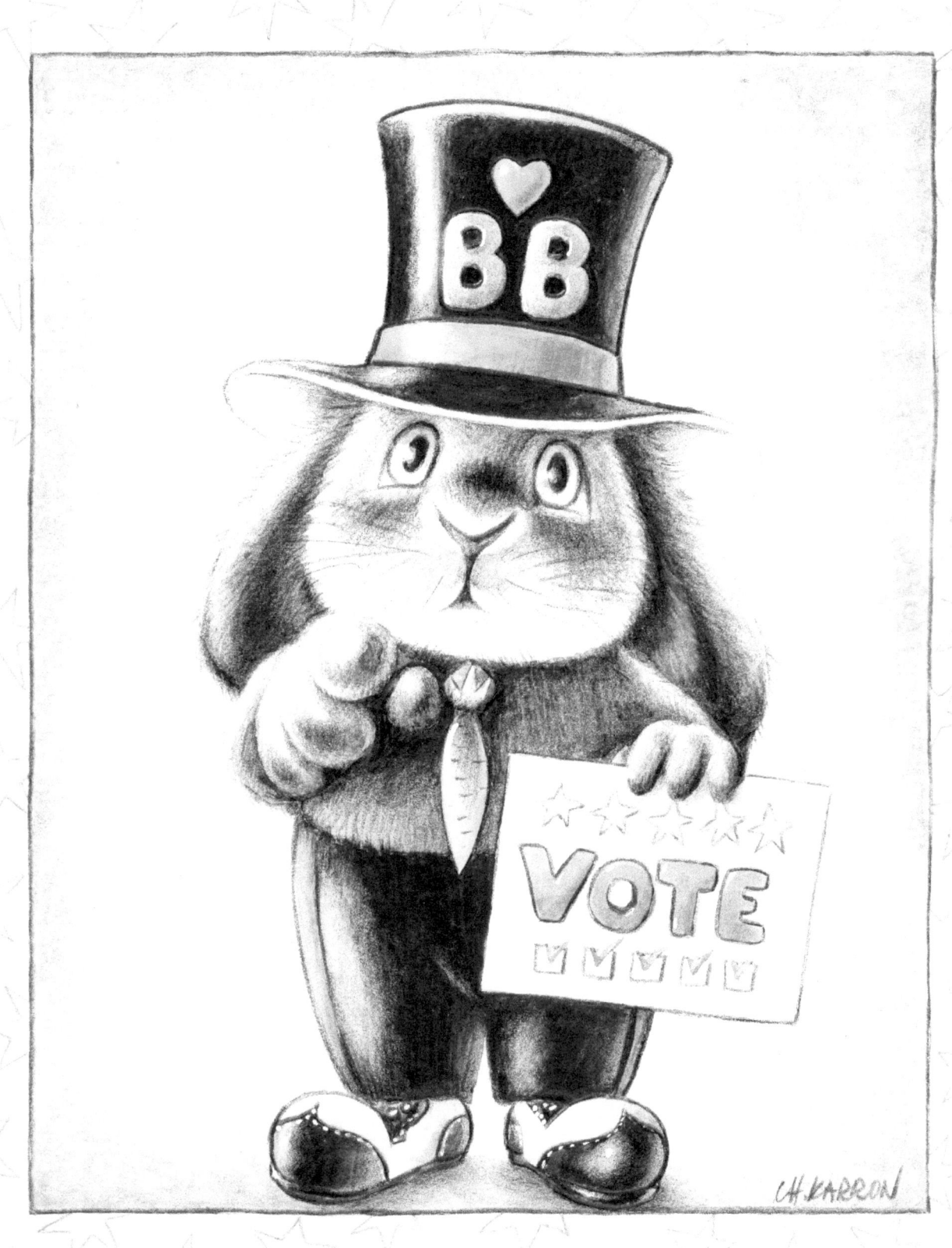

Benny Blue Vote by Christine Karron

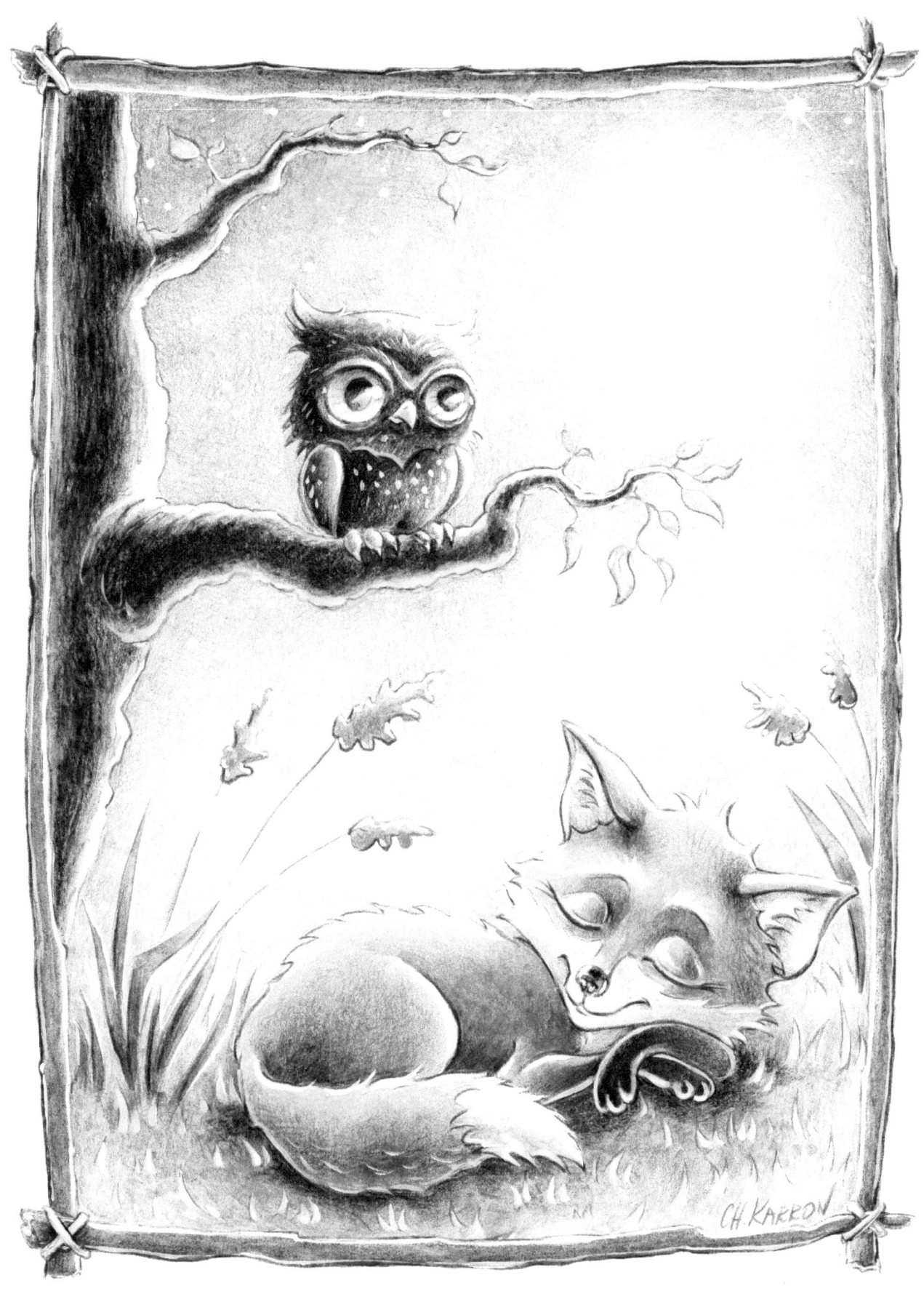

Sleepy Fox by Christine Karron

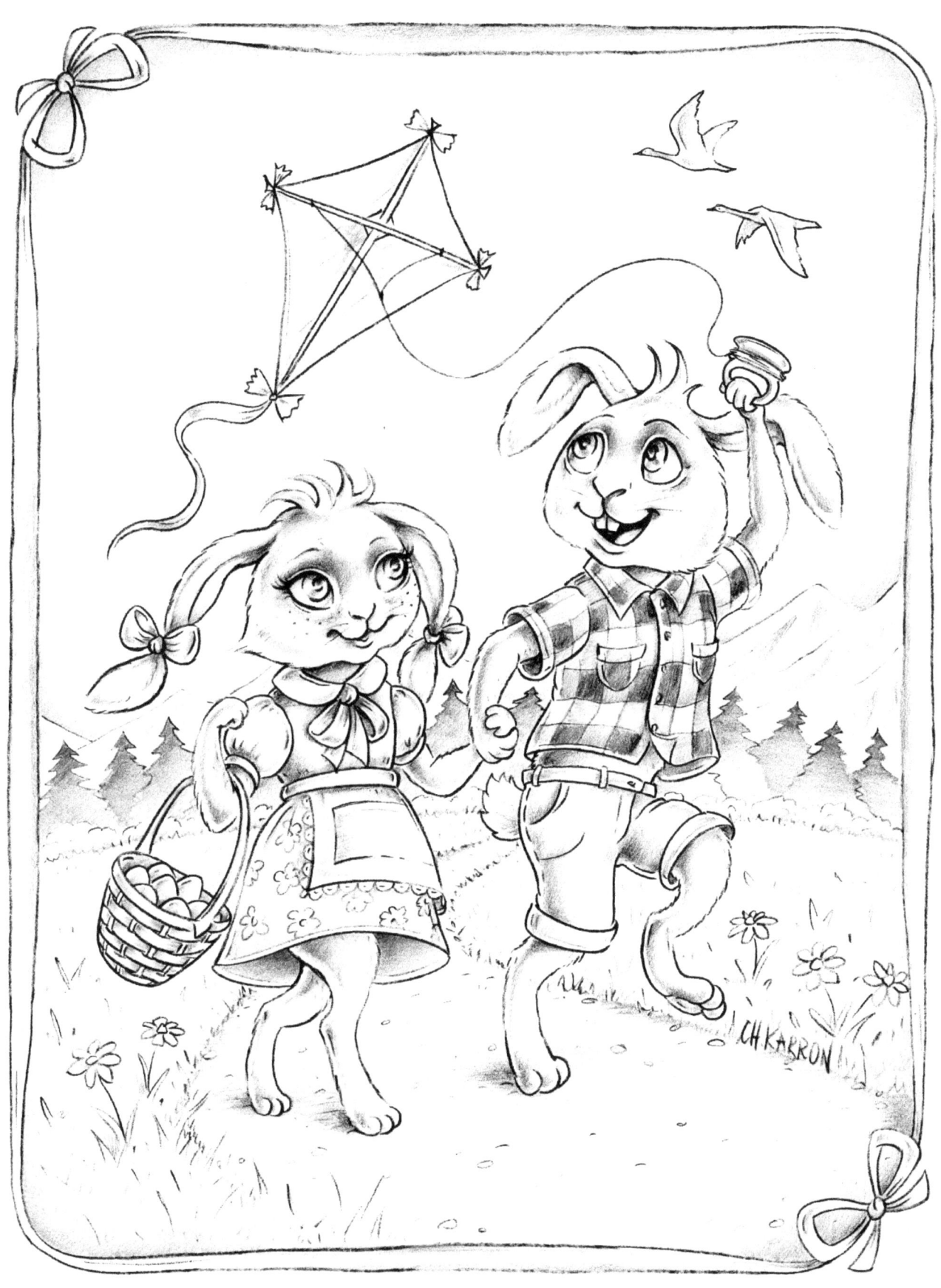

Easter Bunnies by Christine Karron

Christine Karron is an artist and illustrator based in Alberta, Canada.
Drawing and painting has always been Christine's passion. With some formal training, self-education and experience, between raising kids and taking care of her family, Christine has been working as a freelance artist for 20 years now. Her artwork has been sold worldwide, published in books and magazines in Europe as well as in North America.
Christine has illustrated 6 children's books and a few years ago she started the adventure of self-publishing colouring books. Christine loves to create fantasy illustrations and characters with a whimsical, narrative and humorous touch. Working traditionally she uses primarily coloured pencils, ink pens/markers and watercolour on paper.
You can follow Christine Karron on Facebook and Instagram,
or watch work-in-progress videos on her YouTube channel.

Coloring books by Christine Karron:

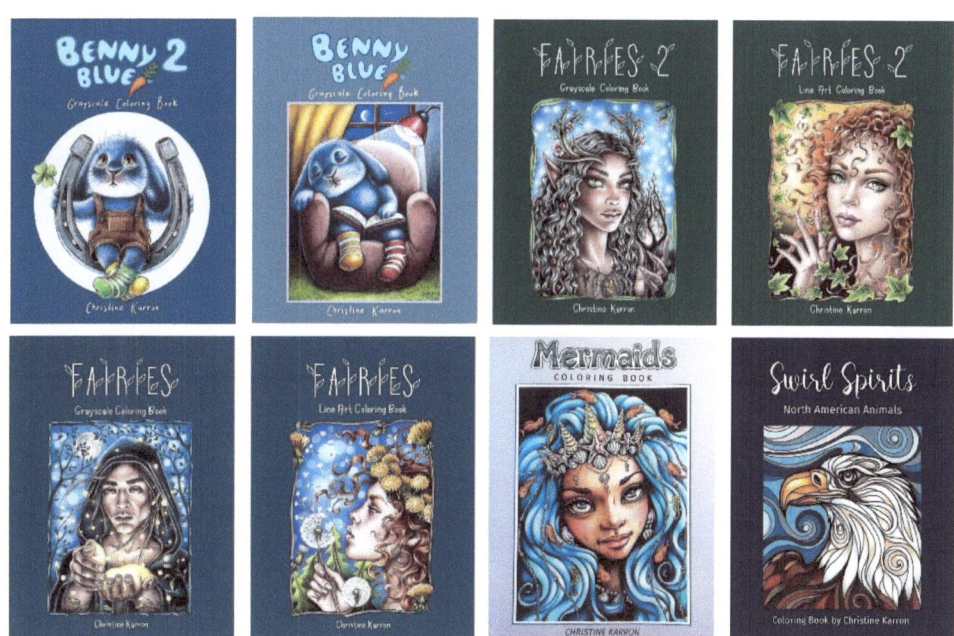

Printable downloads (in PDF format) of coloring books and
single coloring pages are available in Christine Karron's Etsy shop.
Visit www.chkarron.com for coloring ideas, samples and coloring demo videos.
You are welcome to join Christine Karron Coloring Collection Fan Group on Facebook.